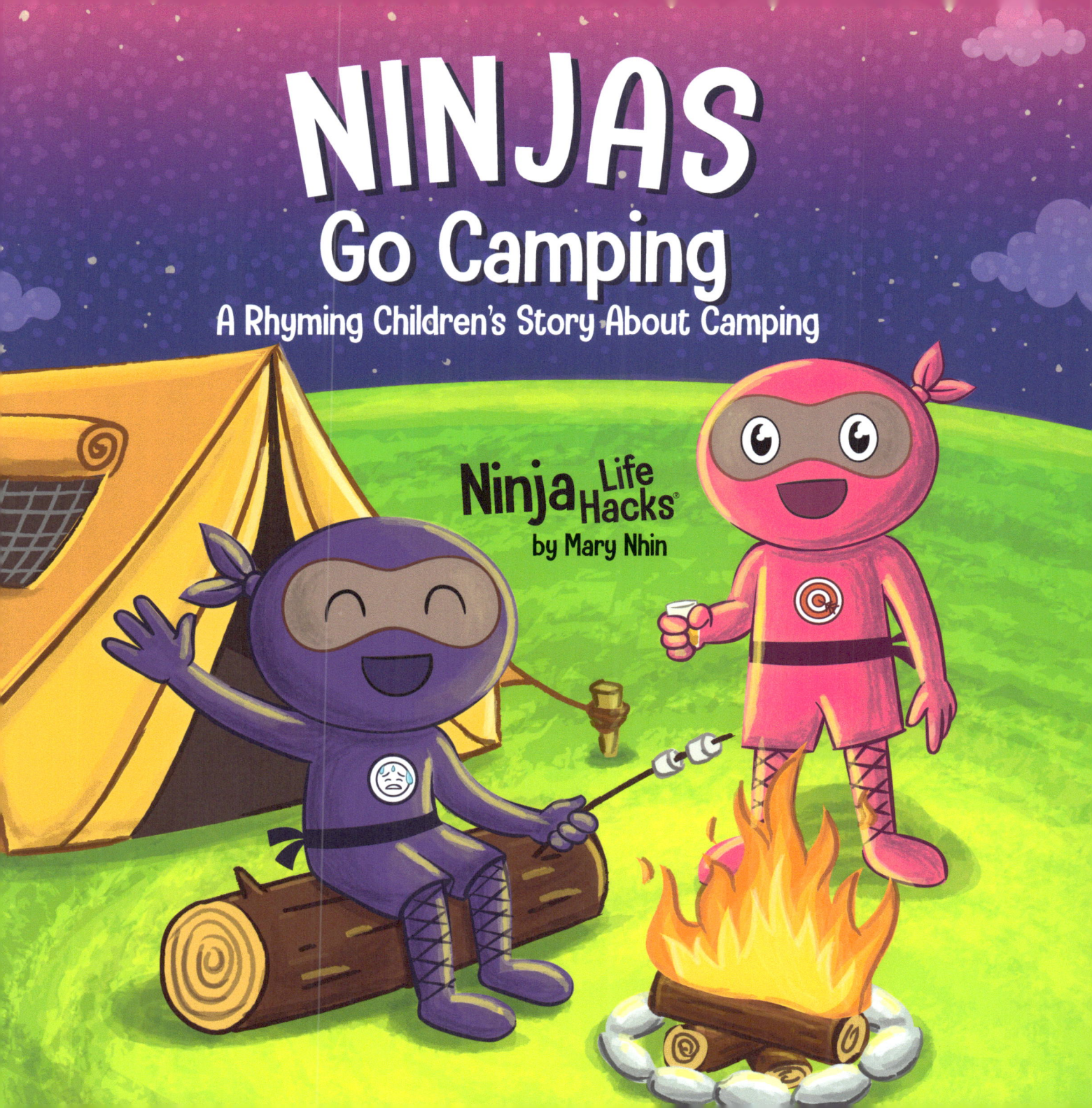

As we drove, I looked up,
And saw some clouds overhead.
'What if it rains on us, Dad?' I asked,
'Can't we stay home instead?'

When we arrived at the campground,
Lots of campers were there.
I began to worry,
Would we see a bear?

And what fun I had with my new friends!
I saw birds and swam in a creek.
And though it was too scary to be alone,
I even played hide and seek!

That night, as I lay down in my tent,
I said with a smile,
'I'm proud of myself for facing my fears,
I think we can stay for a while.'

I love to hear from my readers. Write to me at info@ninjalifehacks.tv and let me know your ideas for my next book!

Yours truly, Mary Nhin

 @marynhin   @officialninjalifehacks    Ninja Life Hacks
#NinjaLifeHacks

Mary Nhin   Ninja Life Hacks   @officialninjalifehacks